BRIDGES, TUNNELS AND ROADWAYS

Ellen Catala

Contents

Rigby®

A Harcourt Achieve Imprint

www.Rigby.com
1-800-531-5015

Introduction

Going from one place to another is sometimes easy. It is just a matter of traveling down a path. But what happens when the path is muddy or when there is something in the way?

How can paths be made easier to travel? How can mountains, rivers, and waterfalls be crossed? Bridges, tunnels, and roadways are the answer.

Bridges

History of Bridges

People have been building bridges for a long time. The first bridges were probably just logs laid over streams. There are many examples of old bridges in Europe and other parts of the world.

This stone bridge was built by the Romans more than 2,000 years ago.

People used ropes to build this bridge.

Long ago in China, bridges used to have places to eat on them. People would stop to have a meal as they crossed.

The ancient Romans also built bridges, and some are still standing today. They built them strong enough for many soldiers to cross over them.

In the United States, covered bridges made of wood were once popular. Wood was easy to get and was much less costly to use for building.

This bridge was built by farmers. They covered it with a roof to protect it from the weather.

Types of Bridges

There are three basic types of bridges—beam, arch, and suspension. Each has a somewhat different shape. Each also spreads out the weight of the bridge and its **load** in a different way.

A beam bridge goes straight across. The weight of the bridge is held up by posts, or piers.

This beam bridge has piers holding it up.

An arch bridge is curved, formed in the shape of an arch. The weight is spread along the arch.

"To suspend" means to hang. A suspension bridge hangs from thick cables that go across the top. The weight is spread along the cables.

This arch bridge spreads out its weight along the arch.

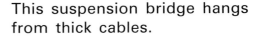

This suspension bridge hangs from thick cables.

How Bridges Are Made

Before a bridge can be built, the land needs to be cleared. Then supports, or posts, must be built to hold up the bridge. Once the supports are built, the bridge can be placed on top. This may require the help of cranes and other big machines.

Sometimes, however, machines aren't the answer. For example, in 1847 a suspension bridge was built over the Niagara River. To run the first line, or cable, a kite-flying contest was held. When a boy's kite crossed the river, it was tied at the other end. This was the beginning of the entire bridge!

This suspension bridge was built over the Niagara River.

Tunnels

History of Tunnels

People may have gotten the idea for tunnels by watching animals burrow into the ground. In Babylonia, more than 4,000 years ago, people built a tunnel under a river. In ancient Rome, people dug tunnels to go under the walls of their enemies for surprise attacks!

Prairie dogs and rabbits dig tunnels to make homes for themselves and to hide from enemies.

One of the first tunnels built in the United States was Pennsylvania's Schuylkill Canal Tunnel. It was opened in 1821, before there were cars, trucks, or trains. What was the tunnel used for? You guessed it—boats.

This tunnel was built for boats, and was one of the first tunnels built in the U.S.

Types of Tunnels

Just like bridges, there are different kinds of tunnels. Some tunnels are dug through solid rock. Others are dug through the soft earth or the sand and mud under a river or ocean. The Seikan Tunnel in Japan, the world's longest tunnel, passes under the ocean.

Some tunnels are built through solid rock.

Some tunnels are started at each end and dug toward the center. The Channel Tunnel, or "The Chunnel," is one example. It was built to connect England and France and was completed in 1994.

The Chunnel connects the people of England and France.

When workers from both countries reached the middle, they shook hands!

Other tunnels are made by digging downward at the center and then out to each side. Still another kind of tunnel is a "cut and cover" tunnel. A cut is made in the ground and then covered over to make the tunnel.

How Tunnels Are Made

Building a tunnel involves digging, blasting, or both. If blasting is needed, holes are drilled and explosives are put inside. After the blast, the rock has to be scooped up and carried out.

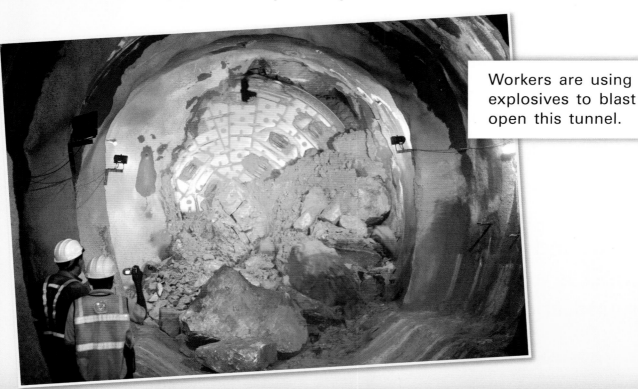

Workers are using explosives to blast open this tunnel.

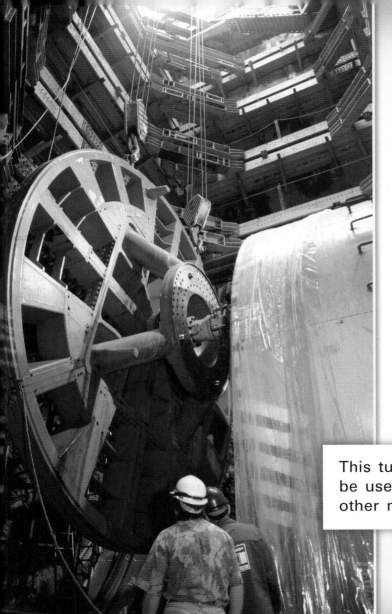

When tunnels are dug, a tunnel-boring machine is often used. This machine digs through the ground, making it much easier to dig tunnels through hard rock. As the digging moves forward, supports are added to the walls so the tunnel won't cave in.

This tunnel-boring machine can be used to chop through rock and other materials.

Roadways

History of Roadways

Before there were roads, people traveled along dirt paths. These paths got very muddy when it rained, which caused cars to get stuck in the mud. People invented roads to make traveling easier and more comfortable.

Believe it or not, early cars sometimes had to be pulled from the mud by horses.

In the United States, one of the first big roads was the Boston Post Road. It connected the cities of Boston and New York. George Washington traveled this road, and so did the Pony Express— bringing mail. Today parts of the road are still used, but now cars race along it rather than horses.

Here is one of the original stone markers that showed riders how far they had gone along the Boston Post Road.

Types of Roadways

There are many different kinds of roads, but they all have one thing in common. They let people go across the land, traveling from place to place. There are country roads, city roads, highways, and superhighways.

The streets in this city were carefully planned to make traveling easier.

Highways help people get from place to place more easily.

In the United States, **interstate highways** connect one state to another. The highways are numbered so that drivers can follow the same road for a long distance. The numbers also help people find highways on maps.

How Roadways Are Made

To build a road, trees, rocks, small hills, and even houses must be cleared away first. Then a ditch is dug, and pipes are laid down and covered with dirt. Pipes allow water to pass under the road, rather than flooding over it.

Pipes are laid down underneath the road.

Heavy rollers press the gravel and rock layers tightly together to form a firm base for the road.

Next the road is built up from layers of **gravel** and small rocks. Finally the road is paved with either **asphalt** or **concrete**. This gives the road a surface that is smooth but not too slippery. After some finishing touches a new road is ready for traffic.

Conclusion

When you put all the bridges, tunnels, and roadways together, you have a transportation system that allows us to go across our great land. This system connects us all as we go to school, to work, and to visit family and friends.

The bridges, tunnels, and roadways we build change our lives, but they also change the way our land looks. Whenever it's possible, we should plan our bridges, tunnels, and roadways to look nice. Then we are adding something pleasing to an already beautiful world.

Glossary

asphalt a type of black, sticky material used to make roads

concrete material made from cement, pieces of rock, sand, and water

gravel broken up rock used for building roadways

interstate highways numbered roads that let people drive easily from state to state

load the weight that a bridge handles when people, cars, trucks, or trains pass over it